Dreaming Lost Bodies Back

Novel Adventures: Explorations in Creativity and Spirituality

Novel Adventures is a single and multi-author book series focused on exploring questions of spirituality, creative practice, and work for the global common good. Works in this series explicitly affirm the importance of imagination and dialogue, providing an opportunity for mutual exploration and learning between diverse disciplines and thinkers. Each volume reflects an embodied inquiry, with the author or authors of a given book exploring a common question from a "novel" perspective unique to them and the expertise they bring to the table. These books will be able to be used in faith communities, in undergraduate classrooms, and in graduate programs as examples of theopoetics-in-action.

The series provides an outlet and archive for documenting work coming from folks who are not formally part of the theological academy and/or may not have completed doctoral, master's, or bachelor's studies. In many instances, such works can provide invaluable insight into understudied or burgeoning areas ripe for exploration in theology or religious studies. We are committed to providing a platform to innovative work that has a practical emphasis and intends to catalyze reflection and material transformation in the world.

Dreaming Lost Bodies Back

Poetry

by Najeeba Syeed

Novel Adventures
Explorations in Creativity and Spirituality

CASCADE *Books* • Eugene, Oregon

DREAMING LOST BODIES BACK
Poetry

Novel Adventures: Explorations in Creativity and Spirituality

Cascade Books
An Imprint of Wipf and Stock Publishers
199 W. 8th Ave., Suite 3
Eugene, OR 97401

www.wipfandstock.com

PAPERBACK ISBN: 979-8-3852-0012-2
HARDCOVER ISBN: 979-8-3852-0013-9
EBOOK ISBN: 979-8-3852-0014-6

Cataloguing-in-Publication data:

Names: Syeed, Najeeba, author.

Title: Dreaming lost bodies back : poetry / Najeeba Syeed.

Description: Eugene, OR : Cascade Books, 2026 | Series: Novel Adventures: Explorations in Creativity and Spirituality

Identifiers: ISBN 979-8-3852-0012-2 (paperback) | ISBN 979-8-3852-0013-9 (hardcover) | ISBN 979-8-3852-0014-6 (ebook)

Subjects: LCSH: American poetry—women authors.

Classification: PS3626 2026 (print) | PS3626 (ebook)

I dedicate this book to my children
Who not only made me a mother
They also taught me what true love is . . .

Left Behind

When i see these bodies

I wonder how did I make it

Why was i left behind?

I call across the space between us
Remembering my mother and her mother before
Asked the same question

One after another
Generations of hope

each new child

A promise for the future

I meant to love you more

when you were here.

I whisper in their ears

Staring at these pictures.

Once moving

Holding On

I tell them,
Leave me

Bind my soul
to theirs

There was never a day
We did not love each other

Surahs, and chapters
Verses and chanting
Prayers and duas

Every language was ours
I want to follow their souls
Go on that great journey with them

When will we meet again?
Where will we hold hands again?
How will I bow, now broken in the humanity
of our chain of existence.

Speak said the child taken to soon
We left you behind so you could carry

Us.

Our stories are there in your hands
We etched them on to your heart
We henna-d them to your feet

Tattooed, forever, you are our forever

You are chosen as we were.

Tell the world who we were, to you
To all.

Tears

I do not believe in tears
They do not bring back what was lost
They do not form what was unformed
They do not speak what tongues are gone
They do not wash pain that is piercing your body
They do not solve the end of love
They do not hold you in one lonely black night after another
They do not comfort the baby crying for her mother
They do not fill the empty chair at the table
They do not confuse all their languages, one sentence in three
tongues
They do not drive me to school and forget my lunch
They do not hug their lover when she grasps for the empty space
On her bed
None of this they do.

But for one minute, they let me hear your voice
And for that minute, maybe I will believe in tears
They are you.

Dreams

I dream of the empty space
Your body left.

Its cut out is on the kitchen floor everynight
How you would sweep as I chopped onion bits onto
The floor.

Why did we get white tiles, i always smear them
Turmeric ridden, you would spill bleach once a month
As if by design, cleansing my culinary sins.

I see you walk into rooms
Your life filling the spaces between people
One body could take over every conversation
Life, liberty and the pursuit of speaking,
You were a champion of the party
Of every party.

Now I walk in alone,
Knowing you won't come in 10 minutes later

No Entrance.
No complexly negotiated exit between the groups of men in one room
And the women in the other.

The good bye at the door
Then the car, then the wave as we left the street

I will never see those times together.
I must live without you, and all the spaces you created

Voices

My voice has
been trapped in my voice
until you set it free

FUTURE POEMS

Am I in Your Future?

We look at each other
I am the past talking to the future

You carry me on your back
strapped in, its never a joyride

What comes next, is it
always made by me?

When did we become enemies?

I think about this question
everyday.

What could i have
done differently?

Was i too soft?
Should I have let go?
Where do I start,

And you begin?

We began

Now we are caught
in inevitability/

Is this course set?

Is there an off ramp my love

When is pain too much
to love each other again?

Your Children

I want yours

at any hour

I want to take them

with me.

They flew so far

Away from us

We look at them, from above

We are the angels now

We carried them here

We let you take them from

The land

A better life, a better place

Oh my beloved

Was it worth it?

Separation

Women know

We must let go to live

We cut each bond

Braid each rope

And sever again

If you hold too tight

When the Pharoah's men come

How will you unclench your

Grip, your metal embrace

of your first born?

His life is of your hands,

Then in the hands of another,

They are Gibran says,

Ours yet not Ours,

God's and God's

Women know,

We must let go,

to live.

Blurred Vision

Mothers do you see

Our children, as

Children.

Or maybe we should ask,

Mothers do you see

Our children,

as

Humans?

The End of a People

Languages die
on the vine everyday
Branches of civilizations
wither in the sun's rays

The fruits of labor
fall down,
Oversweet rich with rot

Men walk on the dregs

Mashing people into mud

As each succumbs to history

Who hears their mourning/mother's cries?

Lament for tributaries of grief.

If a child dies alone,

The last of her name,

Who carries her, Lord?

Who remembers her name to you?

Is she lost forever, her line and lineage

unuttered in heavenly speech?

God calls us down to Earth
Reminding us each tree bends to Him

No beloved of my beloved

She came home
to Me.

The malaika held her gently
caressed her bleeding brown brow
We held her so close her breath
Never stopped breathing.

We are her breath.

Passage of time

I am a wound

born from a long line
of lacerated souls

Someone said,

we were whole once.

I think they were lying.

Memory is not a comfort

Memory is a gaping hole

Where every memory

back, barbed in a mother tongue.

I am a wound

Not the pretty kind

or the very poetic type

I am open, bloody and prone

to explosions.

A volcano soul.

I am a wound

People try to cover me, hide me

under layers, many try

to suffocate me.

They cut the air to my lungs

I creep out from the blankets

Sometimes finger by finger

One visible nail sends many into a panic

I am a wound

Whether you like me or not

I am yours,

You.

A Poem

If you are reading me
You must have found me under love lost
A category it seems common to many
I am never alone in my condition

Words are here to soothe you
Someone wrote me from their own pain
I was caused by their torn soul

If you are reading me
Maybe her pain will help yours
Maybe these lineages of horror
Suffering and paper cuts
On our finger tips as you

Slide through this book,
maybe as your tears wet my page
something will be released

Beloved reader
I cry too for your beloved
Whether a person or your people, lost

we found each other,
Lineages of love

Are greater than family trees
of cruelty.

HOPE POEMS

Broken

Everyday I wake
Take my body in all
Her parts.

I am a seamstress

of pain you forgot

left in crevices

on the back of your thigh

your cackling knees

your dreamy forehead

ripples on your chest
I name your wound

wounded-ness

Generations of silence

break at my fingertips.

Sleep

Someone told me
I need to sleep 8 hours

I can't remember sleep
I can't remember memories

Sleep is a memory
Maybe even a dream

Once I saw a baby sleep,
Hands wrapped in cloth

They were held together
Snuggled into a small space

I wonder what it means to sleep
Without knocks on the door
Disappearances and rains of bullets

Sometimes real
Sometimes living dreams

Someone told me
I need to sleep,

I looked at them,
And asked,

Have you ever been

Awake?

Safety

My love, I kiss your baby feet
We tried to hard to hold on to you
To give you the love we promised God

My love, I kiss your baby fingers
When they would curl around my dupatta
Hold tight, nothing was sweeter

My love, I kiss the hollows in your cheeks
My father gave them to you, his gift, his stamp
On your glorious chubbiness

My love, I kiss the top of your head
From there comes a scent most mothers
Know is anointed by God

I have broken every promise I made to God
To keep you safe,
A-ma-na

The word I violated, the world violated,
a covenant to keep

Your baby body in one piece, together
I tried so hard, to keep you safe,
To keep us together.

My last moment was a shelter
To your baby parts, your body, my beloved

I was gone before you.
I am watching here from my grave

My love, I kiss your baby hands
Holding them, you, me,

Here we are safe,
It is quiet,

We are together.

Witness

Sacred
is the soul
that sees
the pain

Change it with your heart
With your head
With your hand

Sometimes,
All we can do is watch

Not look away
A hundred times,
So we can record those faces
before they fade

A human act is to see another
Human in pain,
And to give them the dignity of your
Face.

Sons of Adam, daughters of eve
Here is our dignity in our face.

Sacred is the act
of witness.

Imperfect.

I saw your story
I shared it
I told another human
I gave them your name

Sacred is your story

I held it as a trust.
I will keep sharing you

You live in these words

What Are Humans But Our Stories?

One day, maybe already
they have made a movie
of our tragedy, found the right person
to play me.

Maybe its going to win an Oscar
Maybe it will trend everywhere
Maybe the brown beauty will look like
Me on Vogue

Maybe you will read about me
in your history books,

Maybe I will be a rallying cry
for new atrocities to be stopped

Maybe I will be woven into a novel
by the author who is writing, about us
not of her own people

Maybe my name will be pressed on the
lips of people protesting.

Maybe.

When you could,
Have saved me,

Why didn't you?

Memories

Remember me dancing
Remember me moving
Remember me loud
Remember me in joy
Remember me cutting a move
across the dance floor
Remember me stomping
Remember me drumming
with my body an instrument
Remember me dreaming
Remember me quiet
Remember me reading
Remember me contemplating
Remember me on the stoop
Remember me braiding my daughter's hair
Remember me squinting in the sun
Remember me leaving my top button, unbuttoned
Remember me in color, deep blue and castle green

Remember

Me.

Come Back for Me

I left you in the back parts of my brain

You always haunt me when I drink my coffee

I left you there on purpose

I left you and I left me both, there.

You know how to pinch my ankles

You know where to punch me hard

You know where to find me.

Slowly, I will come back for you.

Please come, limb by limb

Enflesh, part by part

I cannot handle it all

I am coming back for you.

Without you, I am not me.

The Mathematics of Nations

One day I gain a country,
only to lose another
The one of my dreams,
the other of aspirations

Country over faith
Faith over language
Borders over life
Stamp my body and documents
Claimed and yet rejected all at once
Borders over life
Brown like me lined up
raven headed
seal skinned bodies
you look like me I say
to the instagram feed
Do I claim you,
Do you claim me?
How much must we share
to stake a claim on land
and each others bodies
Borders over life
Boundary crossers were not
always daring, tourists of peak experience
Maybe they were merely
Trying
Forced to choose
Life over borders
Will we?

At the Edge

The edge of a nation
is razor sharp or wool soft
it depends on the papers attached
to your body.
Some crossings are full of
welcome to our country signs
caresses on your pocket urging
out some sweet mementos for
the ones left home.
Some are so barbed, they cut
Deep memories, tattoos across
a baby's skin.
when she grows she will carry
that wire crown on her head as her memento
I want to know why we made
borders, made them our religion?
we choose them over life
Die for them, worship the lines
they contain, hold them liens on the lives of those who are on the
wrong side
I want to know why we drew them first?
Was human imagination hard wired for hurting others?
When did we decide you were you and
I was the other
Mother Earth will cry aloud at the end of her Life.
Quake and pour her secrets forth.
I think one of them will be these
Arbitrary lines
we made on her waist.

She will cry for when she was whole
Roamed across and wild
We caged her
Caged us,
and in the end
Made borders
Our only religion

HUMAN POEMS

Face

My other mother told me to look in the mirror every morning, you will find a person. Speak her name and remind her every morning you are human you are human. Not everyone will understand that you are human. You are not to be afraid when people are afraid of you. I gave you my smile because you will have to charm your way into rooms, past people who meant to keep you out. You will have your grandmother's high cheekbones to cut into the space you were not meant to take up. You will have soft brown eyes that hide a chilly frame steel stone soul that can live through anything. I kissed your eyebrows when you were born so they would not furrow when the eyes of others laid poison on you. You will be a master of disguise of all kinds and never fully let go. I give you freedom, in your mind. There, no matter what you will have words, you will know what is behind that mask and she is so soft, she melts on touch.

That is you,

that is you,

free.

Fire

Do not sleep nor dream without
fire
You were chosen from heaven
descending
to Earth
Gather kindling through the day
You know the sources
that feed you

I know you want
to burn out
Your specks of flame
some days barely blot
out the ink of night

I know you want to
extinguish yourself
other days

To be this luminous
is costly for your soul
You dream aloud at night

Praying for an ordinary light
You were chosen
You know this
Your shoulders heavy with God's
assigned burden.

All we can say,
burn slowly
We need the rest of you soon

No Stories

I am sorry I did not teach you
all the stories
I fell silent at night
when I should have spoken
I kept languages from you
hidden, locked away from your tongue
I did not want you to taste the pain

I gave you nothing.
No inheritance of song
I gave you empty hugs
No mother words
I have you backpacks full
of unknown promises to care

I tried to save you again and again
from the utterances and sounds that
crash against the sea that became my own
Chaos of a life.

One day you will find the map
that was hidden, I am from a land with no borders
Maybe that is why,

I gave you an empty page

Nursing

Mothers are masters of making
these baby humans are cute
helpless, depending on how they are
cataloged by the cruelty in this world.

Some babies are never babies
they are demons from birth
for some eyes, who do not see
Their hands grasp their mothers
scarf, burp and cry softly for the food
God chose for them.

Some babies are never babies
they are left alone to suffer
their losses are not losses, they are gains
for people who live in fear of their humanity.

Some babies are never babies
they are promises of a future where you and i
live together, equal, unhinged from
the past.

Some babies in purgatory
between kindness and cruelty

I pray for you to see
Them, us, all of us…
Human. Babies
at least?

Healing

In the light of love
we still dance.

We call your names
Across the span.

Of time kept
close by clock-less ancestors.

Dream with me slowly

Each body in ours
We are a body

of healers
Spirals of pain
are only the map.

It is the landless dreams
that connect us

Our Earth held us
always

She does not understand
Languages of Separation.

Her seeds are us.
Spread across the soil

We are more than
Scars.

We are more than
Pain

When you look away,
We kept dancing

Valentine's Day

Some great men were martyred to keep war
From the beds of loved ones.
Saints who knew that love, saves
If marriage kept your beloved from war.

What would you do?

Would you give a limb, a sum, a heart
What might the emperor extrat from your body
To keep your beloved in your bed?

Safe, and yet a cost.
No violence but a payment in violence,
Must we hurt ourselves to hear peace?

Forgetful Bodies

Everything is trauma informed
Formed by trauma
Trauma sensitive
Trauma embracing
Trauma traumatized
Re-Trauma
Drama
Some people say leave at the door
I am music that plays only in pain
I want to be a human devoid of humanity
Cold, compressed into time here
Tea bags under the eyes do not remove bags made
By no sleep ever.

When will time end?
My body asks me everyday. Why do you make me alive?

I have no answer, some bodies
Never forget.

WHAT IS SACRED POEMS

Big-Hearted Women

The anatomy of my heart
Is uncharted.
My doctor tries to guess its
proportions
Enlarged, overpopulating
its organic space.

How many more breaks
can it take?
Fissures slight
one day.
Grown into canyons
of pain.

Broken upon brokenness
all the screams are
pressed into her.

Please take my heart
uncut her from me.
She is my revelation
and witness,
Keeping score on inhumanity
Growing bigger by the day

One Day

One day i woke up and realized you do not think of me as human
I tried so hard to convince you
Perfect face, eyes lined just enough to look pretty not scary
Every morning i looked in the mirror trying to be palatable
So you could eat me with your eyes and not throw up

Every night I took off my armor
Laid her down she was not made of mettle
But sweat and smiles
Of disarming earrings and a color palette to please you

No black, no dark colors, pink and barbie
So you can look at me and digest me whole

I tried everyday.
But you kept resisting me
All these years of thinking i was irresistible.

My body broken down

I will walk now into every room.

Your terror comes with the territory.

Holy Books

Dream after dream of prophets
we wait in haunted crevices for your
delivery from evil.

The tribes before you were arrogant
they stood up to God,
their gold lining rivers of pride.

Look up at the sky,
famine is coming,
locusts waiting to roost on your crops.

The Pharaoh is looking for your first born
A boy in a cradle is born,
his mother untouched.

Every story tells another story
buried beneath it.

Who lived to tell these tales,
Weave them into your fabric and mine?

These miserly men
their sins enumerated by verse after verse

And yet every lesson is unlearned

New books are written, not in words

But the mother holding her smothered

Beloved baby body

She is a holy text, unraveling

Dust Upon Dust

I look across the land

You have returned to GOD, too soon

Everywhere is grey

Clay has already come back in its form

We thought you would stay with us,

Your people

Joined God earlier

Holier

than thou.

We do not mean to compete
In this journey

Dust fills in your emptied, shells
of homes.

Where are the prayers for these empty, crushed houses?

On your journey, the souls that filled them

Our lament is carried with you

Our baby malaika, speak to our God

Let him know, we let you go too early.

Stones

I look for signs of God under rubble
How many times have I made this search

Ya-Rabb
Our Rahman
Our Rahim
Our Quddus
Our Salam
Our Mu'Min

Our Lord
Our All Compassionate
Our All Merciful
Our Pure One
Our Source of Peace
Our Inspirer of Faith

My angry cries
Weeping finger
Furious soul

I am not a Denier of You
I am a lover of You

Take this anger
Melt her into something that can feed
Shaking souls left here in these stones

Redemption

This song of mine
Is not mine alone it is woven with the pain you have collaborated on to construct the instruments that wound us up into puppets to animate
We knew what we knew
We saw what we saw
We became nothing of what you made us

Our bones were made the fields fallow
Ready for the machines to rule over our land
We surprised you, becoming the land

We wait there quietly
For the land loved us
Held us,
Made love to us again and again

We cannot be erased
For even the stones laid upon our graves
The salt you strewn in our wounds
The water you flooded our houses with

We floated into it all
The stones, the salt the water

We were of them

We will whisper deep into your dreams

Every breath you take will echo ours you have taken

Number

If you have killed one it is as if you have killed all of humanity.
Qur'an

Once you see one of us as non human, four legs not two

Once you stop seeing one of us us, at all

Once you take one of us and hold our feet over a fire

Let us burn piece by piece

Our skin is not scaly

It was lush, overwhelming in water

Steamed in the sun warm and blooming

Once my skin become faceless

My body useless,

Once one becomes disposable

We have lost.

Repair

Once upon a time a brother killed another who killed another who killed another who killed another killed another brother

I think about that killing chain

How we link it across time

One long strong bond

that first brother created.

For his sins, his father's sins

Who pays?

For killing, once done by his hands was done by so many hands

How can we hold hands after the blood still flows>

Forgiveness

What God redeems does not erase
the rights of other humans
from the infliction of your harm

An ask for forgiveness for
the one you have harmed
is written into the love letter

We send to God.

Use him not as an excuse
to erase harm,
but

as a bridge to

Repair it.

Wombs

God's Angel

visits the womb of every mother
whispers breath into micro-limbs

A tiny heart receives karamah from the Divine

this busy God forgets no one

In our mother's womb

Someone loves us, even if the womb did not

Someone called us into being, every little

Curl of hand, that spongey skin on your toes

Infinitesimal

Flesh clinging for life to that home

Beloved of our Ours,
when you come and visit this micro-
film body

Keep a piece of her heart clean, pure, untouched by humans

Beloved of Ours,

may she be reminded of your gentleness, your love of softness, your embrace.

Beloved of Ours,

soon I will push her into the ether, uncorded

Give her a rope to hold on to Beloved,

that she may remember, once, she was Beloved too.

PRAYERS

With Every Hardship Comes Ease (Qur'an)

I am writing you a love letter God

I am writing you a love letter God

Do not forget us.

Do not forget us

That is my love letter, God.

He is not a believer who goes to sleep while his belly is full while his neighbor is hungry (Prophet Muhammad)

Once upon a time

a country ended.

Since she had no borders to love.

She had not people who were people, yet she was so very peopled.

Are we neighbors only when we have a line that we share.

Once upon a time,

there were no lines,

And a neighbor might come into your tent

no papers, no one chasing them to cut them down to the lines
We drew,

I am hungry,

Do not sleep.

On Me.

Maybe before we can be neighbors, we must be seen as

humans

That my dear, may be our PR problem.

Beware of the prayers of the oppressed, for there is no veil between it and God (Prophet Muhammad)

I flutter every morning, rising words

I am the prayer to God's ears

I am the one who you beat down, broke bones, crushed my soul

What was left my, dignity, my Karamah

Rises

My Dignity Rises

God gave it to me,

you shall never take it

It, me, is inviolable.

You thought in the dead of night

deading us–slowly

We would disappear, but

God is always watching

In these cages without bars

these rooms without walls,

These dreams rise,

We flesh them daily

Our bones rattle

Ring with their song.

This prayer is a song of the living
We live beyond you

Beneath you will never be yours

What your feet touch,

Reverberate,

Sonorous ululations

We do not own the land

We do not own the story

God, is not above it all…

But here walking with us closest in our song

Living, we are here. Gone in flesh,

here in form, dreaming haunted dreams….

We are here, Living.

On that Day some faces will be bright, laughing and rejoicing (Qu'ran)

Our bones were raised up again this Day

Each small broken part resurrected to Perfection

The greatest Former of Formation

Made us in the most excellent of Forms

Humans were a love letter from God

So beloved were to God

We were brought back again, on this Day

I hear your laughter come into my ears

I see your face shining, after the ashen days it carried

I see your body bend in joy, I embrace your vision

Your hips collide with each other.

We were forgotten on Earth.

Yet the Earth she never forgot us.

Laws did not protect us,

Not the ones in books, not the ones they taught, we never rose

to citizenship, maybe even human-ship

This laughter is not evil, nor is it in revenge.

It is from the souls of children, they have come Home.

They are safe in their Creator's abode.

They came from here, plucked from Heaven to join the Earthly family.

Our prayers for thousands of years before,

For Thousands of years to come

Our hopes were carried in their baby cries.

Join your mothers and fathers, your greatest grandmothers.

We have been waiting to see your faces, bright with God's will

and to hear your laughter,

We and God never forgot you.

We and God never let you go.

We dreamt you back, God gave us back your bodies.

and now dear ones, let your souls rest for all their journeys.

You are Home. Amin

Tawakkul

In the hospital wing

where children's hearts

are replaced by other children's hearts

I heard your 12-year-old body screams

Pain upon pain

Pain.

My womb will not forget

you.

Your father would tell me

"Najeeba please don't cry in the shower…

your son is tearing with you out here."

Your eyes did not forget mine.

tremor upon tremor

In our narrow cell room

God was there, I spoke his name

Every breath, calling him to you.

God, take my body, my soul, rip into pieces, spread my limbs across the ocean

Save this one, my son. My one and only.

Sacrifice me, take my life for his.

Forever and ever time, mothers talk like to God

Negotiating their life for their offspring.

God answered and spared us.

How many mothers must speak like this,

Everyday?

Mathematics

The diplomat is talking,
She says 10 deaths from one side equal 1 from another.
Numbers climb until they stop.
One human equals ten for another.
I ask in my mind which won't stop ticking
Who made this math

God said one life is like all living things

God said one life equals all humans

Mystical math

Propped up against this foreign policy arithmetic

Maybe the ones who hold the ropes

of weapons in their hands

FORGOT

their heart

Left behind, sterilized the great halls of our Learning

Math of class
Math of oil
Math where God is forgotten or only spoken of when we hate

Give me a lesson in cracking your code

So that when you look at me, I see your calculus of my body

before it's exploded, did you add or subtract me from

your equation of what you lose or gain from my loss

of

Life?

O Allah, show me the reality of all things as it really is

Lord, grant me the vision to see

What is not seen

To feel what is not felt

Lord, grant me the heart to be broken daily

Make her never lose that ability to be cut in half

Lord grant me the eyes to tear in pieces

When they see the ways war cut humans

Lord grant me the hands to soothe

The loves who have lost their lovers and babies

Lord grant me the head to hold high

As we lose everything that dress humans into humanity

Lord grant me the legs to run to the burning house

To carry the children who cry beyond borders

Lord, grant me the womb to keep making our people

I am afraid one day,

Lord grant me the memory

To hold on to our language, the sounds of our drums beating in joy, the steps of our dance at our daughter's wedding, the smell of the days of cooking outside the kitchen window, the colors i embroider in your wedding dupatta, the ways you fell asleep in my lap tired after a day of running with your cousins up and down the stairs of our house we have forgotten.

Lord grant me the memories that made me

me.

Resurrection

In the flesh you come to me

Flashy

You never loved to be subtle

In the flesh you come to be

Screaming laughter

I remember the bubble we made

In the flesh,

You and Me, Loved and loving

I dream of you walking, jumping on our bed

In the flesh you come to me

Loud and luxurious

You were never subtle

In the flesh, you are always more than

Too much for others.

For me, I wish I had known, I would

Have gotten drunk on you.

Overflowed, every river of your soul

I would have ingested.

When you left me

I hold on to your footsteps

The last ones i heard descending

The last time.

In the flesh,

You were sacred.

Gifts

When a body leaves this Earth

We mean to give it a ritual of love

A Celebration of Life

When all these bodies leave Earth,
So many they don't have names
Some no faces.

Holy water

I dream of flushing over the limbs

You are in your return to our Divine

I wash your body, slowly imagining it whole

I don't have the gifts of your family name

I cannot read it on your back

I wash your body

I can give you this dream of sanctification

A dream to clean your earthly garment and prepare your soul for heaven.

God will welcome you.

I have for you, dreamt your body back into its form

I saw you holy smiling laughing crying holding your baby in your arms you were so beautiful so happy so full of life that my dream burst

God is waiting for you.

www.ingramcontent.com/pod-product-compliance
Lightning Source LLC
LaVergne TN
LVHW090535110826
845146LV00003B/1114

* 9 7 9 8 3 8 5 2 0 0 1 2 2 *